GOLDEN AX

ALSO BY RIO CORTEZ

CHILDREN'S
The ABCs of Black History (2020)

GOLDEN AX

RIO CORTEZ

PENGUIN POETS

PENGUIN BOOKS

An imprint of Penguin Random House LLC
penguinrandomhouse.com

LIBRARY OF CONGRESS CATALOGING-IN-PUBLICATION DATA
Names: Cortez, Rio, author.
Title: Golden ax / Rio Cortez.
Description: [New York] : Penguin Poets, [2022]
Identifiers: LCCN 2021037007 (print) | LCCN 2021037008 (ebook) |
ISBN 9780143137139 (paperback) | ISBN 9780593511107 (ebook)
Subjects: LCGFT: Poetry.
Classification: LCC PS3603.O7843 G65 2022 (print) |
LCC PS3603.O7843 (ebook) | DDC 811/.6—dc23
LC record available at https://lccn.loc.gov/2021037007
LC ebook record available at https://lccn.loc.gov/2021037008

Printed in the United States of America
1st Printing

Set in Mentor Pro
Designed by Sabrina Bowers

For the Howells, who went west

Now note the great white expanse of the great Salt Lake, as it lies glistening in the rays of the setting sun, and think of the stories you have heard of it until the conductor brings you back to earth . . .

—**Nat Love**

Author's Note

Much like the way Afrofuturism seeks to envision a future for Black people at the intersection of imagination and science fiction, a future that also seeks to remember the Black past, in many ways *Golden Ax* hopes to find its place and definition as a work of "Afropioneerism" or "Afrofrontierism"—terms that describe and inform my family ancestry and experience. This work is autobiographical, but it is also a work of imagined history. These terms approach my experience of girlhood in Utah, wondering how we came to be there, feeling singular in a place where I knew we had been for generations. Continuing to ask myself, "How does a story begin?," the question became an obsession. This is a question so many ask, whose histories are cut short by the design of transatlantic slavery. I no longer wondered to myself whether aliens possibly put me on Earth, smack-dab in the Wasatch Mountains, or other systems of sci-fi that I transposed onto myself as a child. Eventually, the question became an urge to mine the hidden history of the Black West, and to tell the story of how we came to settle that frontier, both physically and spiritually. The poems in *Golden Ax* reflect the outward and earthly landscapes of the Afrofrontier, and the inner, cosmic imagination of the Afropioneer.

My family was once enslaved in Louisiana. After Reconstruction, the first generation that was free from enslavement went West, perhaps inspired by the California Gold Rush. This migration included my second and third great-grandfathers, Paul C. Howell, who became the first Black police detective in Utah, and his son, Abner Howell. Abner was an early Black convert to the Mormon church, a decision others in our family would not make. My family came to Salt Lake City around the time that the African American newspaper *The Broad Ax* was published, which was at some odds with the LDS church. At the time, Abner's testimony to the church became an important narrative for the church in their efforts to appeal to more Black congregants. Abner's conversion created complex tensions around race and faith that remain in our family today. It wasn't until 1978 that Mormons allowed Black men to hold priesthood, before which Black Mormons were not allowed to participate in or enter some of the church's most sacred practices and spaces.

I learned much of my family's history from shared memories and a paper pamphlet published in the 1950s and 60s called *The Story of the Negro Pioneer*, by Kate B. Carter, and from a self-published book written by my great-great-aunt Byrdie Langon, titled *Utah and the Early Black Settlers*. I'm grateful for these records.

My family were Afropioneers and they embodied the Afrofrontier. Over a century later, I am claiming this name and this space for them. The land where Utah exists haunts our story, but we are even more vast. And we know that because we imagine ourselves into existence.

Contents

FRONTIER ELSEWHERE

SPACE BETWEEN MOUNTAINS

Far Enough

Byrdie Lee Howell Langon self-published *Utah and the Early Black Settlers*, a short book about her life and the Black community in Salt Lake City, Utah, and was honored with these words by her Bethel AME pastor, Jerry Ford, in 1969:

We say we love you
not only for what you are
but for what you are
when we are with you
we love you
for putting your hand
into our heaped-up hearts
and passing over
all the frivolous and weak things
that you cannot help
but see there
and drawing out

all the beautiful things
that many
have not looked far enough
to find

Covered Wagon as Spaceship

Standing unseen in the little bluestem,
curious and not quite used to living,
I consider whether it's aliens
that brought Black folks to the canyons, valley.
Standing in the great evaporation
of a lake, holy dandelion for
eyes, full and white and searching the landscape
for understanding: how do you come
to be where there are no others, except
science fiction? I am a child feeling
extraterrestrial; whose history, untold,
is not enough. Anyway, it begins with abduction

UFO, for Instance

When the hole between blue spruce widens

and twists into a cosmos   when the wild

lilac and campfire atomize   and night hangs their smokes

across its belly   when in the clearing you are certain

you are not lonelier   but there is a lifting in you

where other knowing rises too   and divides you from the bone

in your feet to the fat   round your heart and leaves you

surrounded by your own   breath you emerge from

and watch vanish and think   the night ate it ate your knowing and how

could anyone know any more   you might as well look out

into the clouds of long pine that hang   brambled and

orange in branches   you listen for howling but none comes

North Node

According to her, I appeared to my mother in an in utero vision and told her my name. Before I chose my mother, all day long I ran my fingertips along the slick backs of cutthroat trout and gathered water from Millcreek into a sapphire pail. I waited for her. In the distance, there was a blue bull surrounded by lilies.

She loves me, so she bore me underwater. I'm here to learn a lesson. I spent my other lives in the Nevada desert, where I only did what felt good. *What could that mean?* I reconcile the pleasure in lying naked on the hot sand of the Mojave, watching the braided muscles in a horse's hind legs with the ocean nowhere, a frying chest on the hood of an idle car. So comes a lesson, I'm here to cut the scorpion from my throat. Even though it has dragged me through sweet darkness and time. Even now, in the stillness of home, in love and full of wine, it wraps its eight legs around me. Even through the lilies, it sets its many eyes on me and, suddenly, longing

Like a Suggestion

The antelope start dying,
of all places, on Antelope
Island. Our two greyhounds
startle in their sleep and walk
together toward the window.
I've heard wolves are hunting
bison, even though it's spring
and there are easier things to kill.
Cowbirds abandon wooden
fences. They say Atlantic salmon
haven't returned to their cribs
of fresh water. The cat stands still
before an open door to the house.
I move to put my hand behind
her ear and she runs.

I Have Learned to Define a Field as a Space between Mountains

If I remember a field where I stroked the velvety hound's-tongue and cracked its purple mouth from stem and it is not a memory, then what were the limits of the field?

Sometimes we are driving south toward Zion in a crowded truck with my mother and we pass the same red wildflowers until someone says, "Indian paintbrush, Rio, haven't you seen them before?" And, have I?

Other times I pose in front of giant flor de maga, its soft petal saucers larger than my head. My father fixes one behind my ear and says something in Eyeri but for what photograph? I am a conjoined hibiscus-headed twin, except I'm local.

I braid the long hair of the willow and like a young warrior I swing across the canal bed by the braid. *By the rivers of Babylon we sat down and wept when we remembered Zion. There on the willow trees, we hung our harps. How could we sing the Lord's song in a foreign land?* I read this once in Sunday school, tripping on it.

In any field I am certain I can be seen by someone. How couldn't I? When I'm blood-divided one hundred ways, when I pray to the God called DO NOT BOARD THE SHIP, when I'm protected by so many masters of the vine. They must be in here somewhere? They must see me this far into the desert, it can't be that I am alone here. I search behind the cattails, I scramble the wood. Has it gotten darker?

A child and all I can see are houses. Every house is a rambler with a plastic snake full of sand or a well that isn't really a well. Every house is on a street named after the Ute tribes. I'm in Ute Country, in the field to fly a cheap kite, but it gets caught in pine sap. I walk home but not without pocketfuls.

The Idea of Ancestry

After Etheridge Knight

I am in a sweet place
standing in Millcreek
on a road
in its canyon
and this sweet place
has also been the sweet place
of my people

I am staring
into the water
my grandmother fished
with a rod and a line
I am standing
near the head
of a timber trail
felled by grandfather's
grandfather
I am listening
to the aspen
its green coins
singing in the wind
and I know it sang
just like this
for them

I am standing
right at the center
of its singing
the same sound
heard by black bears
or the calf of a moose
lying even sweeter
in the yarrow

showing we can be moonless
and shining in wildflower

I know this timber
was once a house
my mother's grandmother's
mother's hammer in hand
everything
throttling backward
toward me
through time
a timber roof
that has kept the frost
from coming in
and stinging my babies
we made that
for ourselves

I consider choosing
there are times
when it is a joy
to remember
I like to think about my people
drinking fresh buttermilk
from the chosen farms
of their other people
all of us gazing
back at the house
framed by our future knowing
filling up on fresh tomatoes
and after
maybe lying like the silk calf
in the deerwood and the aster
and never-ending

Driving at Night

For Laquan McDonald

I think it's quails lining the road, but it's fallen birchwood.
What look like white clouds in a grassy basin, sprinklers.
I mistake the woman walking her retriever for a pair of fawns.

Could-be animals. Unexplained weather. Maybe they see us
that way. Disappointed, the closer they get. Not quite ready to let it go.

I'm Forced to Imagine There Are Two of Me Here

To fit in   we practice not dancing   I pull her hair against our head and burn
    the water out   she sucks in the lip of our belly

I call her Rio   say Rio   remind them of our one white   grandmother
    do what it takes   to make them think   we are like them

Because it is a risk to want us   we close the bedroom door   she reaches under
the blanket   It's just   me Rio   and   The Dark
    I spit into our hand   and touch her

Sometimes she bites our lips   to make them smaller   we refuse
    to dance   we do what it takes

I let her drive Little Cottonwood Canyon   It is night   we hit a deer   breath
from its nostrils clouds the windshield   It feels like there could be more
    of us somewhere   she opens the car doors   we show each other mercy

take the same bite of a cracked rib   blood from her mouth I move to kiss the animal

I learn to shoot a bow

It is no River Jordan that flows here
between the railroad tracks and the back porch.
It's a canal. Not unlike my mother:
low as it want to be and fullest when
it rains. Existing for however long
without a name, and singing
under a timber bridge that we built. We built that.
Isn't that our story? To be denied
the beginning. I cross the bridge to shoot
a sapling bow my grandfather has carved.
He helps me aim into cardboard flats stacked
against the willow. I guess this is where
I am Orion. With two birth stories.
In one story I come from a sea god
with the forest as my mother, and in
the other, I have no mother at all

Partum

Just as close   to living   as you are   to disappearing   knowing
my limits   you locate   the tender spots   without.
        To be batter and rind

maybe I've hidden   my feral self   even though   I was certain   I was wild
I'm now certain   it was vanity

here I pace   cut open   drinking thistle and yolk
expecting nothing   determined to live

you   Little God,   Oldest Friend
who summons milk   and hair from the follicle   who moves my teeth   and makes
me bleed   it is not a joy   but joyful   to have been   brought
this close
to the earth

haven't we touched hands before?   in the bright red towns of my youth
in Loa or Escalante   where I thought   we were only passing through
was it you at the counter   serving me sarsaparilla   in a cool brown bottle
remembering me?

Marion's 1982 Chevrolet Citation

If I board her   it means pulling open her heavy sails the steel
that gravity throws shut on my calves   good thing
I'm quick to leave

She must be virtuous because there is nothing hidden in her
going   not the power in her closing doors nor the ignition
and its triumphant refrain

even idle, she disrupts   she rests in the cool shade
of a basketball hoop   I stare from my parents' living room window
how the mulberry tree wreaks its havoc on the driveway

all my friends call her The Killing Machine   how else
could she have lived this long and look so good   Marion says
it's like she's been asleep for me

I am days from my sixteenth birthday   I cover her
hatchback in cosmic fish and press
my foot down where do I go   I wonder without them

the chrome of the dashboard reflects the canyon sun
I see myself in fraction   my wristwatch as I pull the radio knob
eyebrow cocked as I adjust her mirrors

A Class Distinction

I start to say

Once,

I left the mountains,

the Wasatch and Oquirrh

talking aloud

I question the spelling

in my head

I've never been sure

It's possible

I wasn't born from mountains at all

but a valley.

What is lower

than a valley?

Once,

I left the strip malls,

I grew up in a long drive-thru line

sipping diet cola from a bent straw

when I talk about mountains

I am being romantic

about the valley

I worry

you'll unmask me

I've always been that way

lying

just a little

on the Berber carpet

squashing summer ants

the TV telling me everything

Salt

I slip the silksac of my body   and walk out   onto the flats
the air a machine   sucking earth into fragments of white   absorbing heat
     finding me

I kneel at the shore   I reach into the lake   it is red   as a halt
     I reach into the wound of it   I drag out   its string of bones
and now I am two   times the dark

I crush skeletons   of artemia underfoot   I eat eggs   in stasis the dead   lake idles
the city   surrounds   what weapons we are   I fold the net of my shadow   I hold it
     as evidence

Emancipation Queen

"Emancipation Queen" was a historically Black beauty pageant in Utah.

It's true
that beauty
can be a tool
dually wielded
    robin's egg
who would know
come from a red-
breasted bird
    taffeta gown
named for what
the body made
its blue
    but not the maker
or the blue
from which come
the robin
    is that emancipation
to leave beauty behind
    a Black girl
    on a stage
    inside the egg
of a robin
    a Black girl who is
a robin
repeating the question

As Cain

Until 1978, Mormons maintained that in a spiritual "preexistence,"
Blacks were neutral bystanders when other spirits chose sides during a
fight between God and Lucifer. For that failure of courage, they were
condemned to become the accursed descendants of Cain.

I think of the earth that drank Abel's blood
as I uproot foxtail from the garden.
Earth, not passive, but cursed by God, having
accepted death, and maybe, even, hoped
to grow from it. And Cain said to Abel,
"Let us go to the field." I cut my own
thumb on a weed. I carry out a strict
ritual of healing: cold hose water and then
most Holy: mouth. Tell me, what mark has God
given me? I am paraphrasing here
when I say God told Cain to rule over
his own longing or else restless wanderer
shall he be on earth. First curse, then blessing.
God's always changing his mind about us

To Salt Lake, Letter Regarding Genealogy

After Charles Olson

No shore no shore   backed against a paradox of water   where snow

collects in valleys and we drink

what melts, I, risen from one break   in the endless

salt flat.   I have had to build. O! how I have built for you!

See how I have come, Salt Lake, with my thousand faces of the void!

My face night with no stars,   my face waves

in night sea.   I was born to work.

My mother, crow-headed goddess, called me dust and trusted

I'd become.   I changed for you! I became

a quarry in Big Cottonwood. Later, I was born

in uniform and carried a pickax in my throat.

I stole the mountain's sandstone and it wasn't good enough

so I took its quartz instead and told you   "pray by it." I,

Guard-thing of the White city.   How would you pray without me!

I was born with a sore head from a perm   and swaddled in pages

from The Good Book.   I was a decoy.

I pretended not to know my many names.

I did the work of believing with you.

I was born on swamp property   the woman who bore me was an animal.

We were both animals, then.

I covered your wagon with canvas   and I found you.

THE NEGRO PIONEER

Self-Portrait in a Tanning Bed

It's February and I am the only Black
girl at Future Tan Tanning
Salon I laugh when I enter
my private room and see an African
mask above the clothes racks I am
getting tired of irony naked
climbing onto the plexiglass and
hearing it creak I wonder like any
other moment alone what if I die
like this what if the plastic gives
and torched by two dozen ultra-
violet glass rods I gently close
the canopy of the Sun Capsule Super
Cyclone 350 wrapped in its purple
cylinders of light I can see myself
reflected back with tiny goggles at first
I think I look like a reverse coon with huge
black eyes but I like the way I look
darker and like a time traveler how
my breasts must sometimes appear
like this to my lover I think I'm sad
or something worry how much time
has passed since I've been here

Black Annie Hall

in a black wool hat
and black suspenders
in line to see *Within*
Our Gates again

with khaki slacks
and an afternoon free
Black Annie has trouble
hailing a cab
after seeing her analyst

on her roof,
Black Annie
drinking white wine
after tennis
and dewy

Black Annie, living alone
calls for help to kill
a black widow spider
in her bathroom

Black Annie's white
boyfriend asks her
not to smoke
that marijuana cigarette
in bed and out-
of-body

Black Annie is bored
so she takes adult courses
and can't decide
between philosophy
and poetry

lucky today, Black Annie
driving eighty on the West
Side Highway with the top
back, hair unmoved

An Ancestor Maybe

Sleep drags from me. I'm living on the top floor at 176th Street & Audubon. Rain falls through the hallway roof, no matter how many times we ask to patch it, turns the marble steps slick as king snakes. The apartment is dark. Behind me the AC whirs and pigeons roost upon it, snagging their claws in its slats. Cooing in unison.

There's a man I don't know at the foot of my bed, dressed to go dancing. My body cool as a gun. His benevolence washes over me and we look, us both, at the other for some time outside time. I show him one version of my Arawak face and there are no matters. We are neither. The night pigeons settle on the vent, make sounds I'm certain of.

Black Mary Wilkie

in *Manhattan*
we all have two-
bedroom apartments
on the UWS
I eat lox
on the Sabbath
I'm a Black girl
with a dachshund
I feel safe enough
to take night
walks with
my skinny lover
so many dawns
I've spent at the East
River, watching
the sun take flight
above the "watchtower"
I'm free midday
and answer
my landline
once–
I got caught
in the rain
it led to a stolen
kiss instead
of a blow-dry
the planetarium
is strangely lit
and filled
with the universe's
few answerable
questions
biting my nails
I think
of that scene
with the lobster

Double Threat

The street narrows, becomes a black prism
Do you want to fuck her?
I am asking you at the crosswalk
I'm loose-lipped and beat-skipping
we've just come from a dinner party
we've been drinking cheap wine
it seems like we float to the corner, like
one of those moving sidewalks at the airport
we stop on Irving Pl and Eighteenth Street
faded, I'm starting to forget
weren't you looking at that pretty gap-toothed girl
in the red dress, weren't you exchanging glances?
I'm trying to prove to one of us
that you cannot want me
trying to get you to say it
you say *how pathetic* instead
I feel a red surge, it flushes my face
I spit at the sidewalk near your feet
I've never done that before, we're both stunned
a white woman with bags of groceries asks
am I alright
looking at our Black faces, further shadowed
beneath the eaves of someone's town house
I say *Yes.* Back in Millcreek my mother
is avoiding a full-length mirror, the white woman
gets a little closer, she asks again. Smaller than before
I repeat *Yes, thank you, please, yes*

Forgetting Is to Heal

On Tenth Street
my Aircast kicks a pink pacifier
I grip any rail sleeve-first
when I get home and take it off
lean the crutches on the wall
undo all that Velcro and peel
the sock away
my foot is yellowish and soft
like no other skin on me
after showering once
it kept rubbing off like
it could all just wipe away
if I wasn't afraid of that

there is a row of single shoes
in better condition than their pairs
these pins when I step down
at first I think it's pain but
not exactly not exactly
is how I balance now
in my kitchen with or without you
I wake up each morning
and I have to remember it

is broken
think what a cinch how I could
place both feet over the bed
and pull on pants one leg at a time
but that's just something
sleep does to us for a little while

It's Like That Scene in *Annie Hall* Where Annie Leaves Her Body

and sits beside the bed   how I'm certain I'm across from me on the 1
train and   when we get into the cab   how I watch myself ride shotgun
and I think Annie starts to knit   or maybe does a crossword   could be
I keep nodding yes   what's important is that she is two
Annies that   what reaches one   not reach the other   that the body
knows   indifference   I ghost steady through the hole in my mouth   I watch you struggle
with buttons on my dress   I keep nodding   yes I fill in   some box
with pencil letters

Black Fragments

I.

Leaning on the subway door   train rushing   between 59th street & queensboro plaza   I think
we're underwater   under roosevelt   island   or something   pitch-black
oil over glass   window   suddenly the door disappears   I'm sucked into the pitch

II.

I force my teeth into a yellow pear   pulling the flesh from my mouth   all but my molars
remain
stuck in the fruit   lined in a row like glaciers   some glossy stonehenge
my mouth   a black gate

III.

Showering   water pours from its nozzle   into my knotted hair covers   my toes their
toeprints   impressions of my mother's deepdarkwomb   pressed into the tile
an instant   all of it familiar

Ritual of Witness

Driving around our Harlem block to look for street parking. I'll circle a long time to get a spot on Convent, where the Callery pear trees steal a little piece of the lamplight and I get to peek into the tall windows of other people's townhomes. Limestone and terra-cotta facades with varying resuscitations.

With each revolution of the block, a figure emerges, or goes: a dog rushing toward the invisible presence of an earlier dog, a lover ringing a buzzer and checking their reflection in a glass door. I am a corner rounder. I see the man who always notices me first, arms akimbo outside of Price Dream. I think of an empty lobby. A child asleep now in a stroller at the crosswalk, whose mother is waiting for the same light to turn. I am a red light lasting. No such thing as a safe distance. Any detail to be a balm or a fever, returning a little later.

Maternal Instinct

I can hear all the wind chimes in Harlem (from the oldest elm with no plaque on 154th Street to that weird store run by Ms. Dee where she sells her ex-husband's records and ties)

and I can hear the elaborate stream of radiator water, boiling and climbing into our most intimate spaces and warming us. My fur, in the sun, roaming our bed in blindness.

I allow it to light me up. I'm a light. Fed by an other light. The cries of a child, suddenly amplified. I can't tell whether I want to run toward them or stay right here.

Conduction

The beginning has a sound. So that when I hear you take a gulp of breath, my hair stands on its ends. And I turn around. So carefully. I don't really want to see.

Once, while you waited for me to put on my shoes, standing a few steps down on the landing so that we could talk face-to-face, you vanished. Where do you go without me? Gripping on to your shirt to keep you from falling backward down the stairs, and failing, I cried out for the neighbors. No one heard.

In a Hollywood movie about Harriet Tubman, they depict Harriet as having protective visions from God. In one novel, in which she is a character, she time travels. It is called "conduction." A biographer says Emily Dickinson rarely left home because of her "spells"; confined to a room at her father's house, where I like to imagine she might have written "Hope is the thing with feathers."

I think of us, postcoital and sharing a glass of tap water. We are parents now. We are watching the last scenes of an intense TV show; someone is finally speaking up for themselves. I turn to you in recognition. But it's not you anymore. I fall with your falling body to the couch.

We might as well be falling into the river where Dana finds herself in *Kindred*. You are Rufus. And I'll do anything.

Black Lead in a Nancy Meyers Film

Aging, at all. I want that. And to fall
perhaps most honestly in love
beside the ocean, in a home I've paid
for by doing as I like: drinking good
wine, dusting sugar over a croissant, or
the stage play I'm writing myself into.
Aging Black woman in neutral summer
turtleneck. Known. And jogging. Lonesome
enough. Eating homemade lavender
ice cream, the moon blooming
through the kitchen window. The distant
sound of waves. Learning
French as a second language.
Votre pâte merveilleux, I smile back.
And then, just like that! Falling, cautiously,
for my busy, middle-aged lover,
who needs me, but has never truly seen me
until now. Our Black friends, celebrating
with hors d'oeuvres. Our Black children,
growing older.

What Begets What Begets

Everything is a ring. I am working on a belief
that starts like that: everything
is a ring, a cycle, it has

the illusion of progress

＊

I woke up blue, so all day long I tried
to make the world blue around me

＊

I heard in a movie once that hurt people
hurt people. Now I always say that
when I am comforting unhappy friends.
I curve the ring so not even I can see it
how it winds right back to itself, loops
right around me when I think
it must be going
I say to myself: look at this sad fool

＊

I am always explaining myself to my lover
I say to him: there are two kinds
of knowing. Some knowing is as close
as my own palm, I don't even know
I know it. I love my mother and my mother
loves me. Other knowing gets submerged

＊

Beauty always strikes me when I consider it leaving and am hurt by it
how now light enters through the curtains at dusk and I find it beautiful
because it is about to change

One layer of that knowing is of the self.
Isn't it like that for everyone? Sometimes
the ring comes round and I feel I don't deserve a thing.
Then I do the work of knowing. I see myself
reflected in the bathroom mirror, it's been a long
day and I'm alone, my hair pulled into a tight chignon,
and I know better by looking at me next to nothing, compared
to nothing, and I say thanks to someone out there

FRONTIER ELSEWHERE

The Creature Describes Her Own Hands

Not
a black ladder

Not quite holding
a painted bow

Wrapped in cotton
and playing the piano

The way they always
almost

I can't stop singing
folk songs about you
And by you
I mean
anywhere but here

A paper map
shaved to ligament

I remember
engaging the bowstring

I need them

I would do anything
to stop singing

The way you release
And soak them in prayer

I don't know any other way
to unlace the knot

Questions of the Last Relative Slave

For Paul C. Howell

What about the trees

    Would he rejoice after storms

    Finding peace in their boughless husks

    Butchered by the wind

Then, did he love the wind?

Écriture Féminine

I was selfish enough
that you were born

      now you watch television
      pumped with my funny blood

I forget myself sometimes
and look at you too long

      I am underloved and braid
      your hair anyway

I copycat the way
a mother does but

      like a mother I'm mostly
      in love with the me in you

Black Frasier Crane

As lonely
in her overthinking
and as forgiven
Black Frasier Crane
is a woman in a multi-
generational household
with more than enough
square feet

Black Frasier has
a small staff
but she treats them
"like family"
she has a soothing
radio voice and reserved
parking at both her condo
and the office

Black Frasier complains
about little everythings
because what is more
important than the fine
dusting of cinnamon
on the perfect ratio
of foam to espresso
except the knowing
that you and
only you
have the sense
to complain

And who else
could understand
but a sister
two Black Cranes
in custom Italian suits

joking about Freud
Isn't this the hardest
work? To be happy

when you already
have everything
to have so much
you give some up
not away
but to the beast in you
that just takes
and takes until
there are no more
brûlées and no more
canapes just the mind's
endless narration

The End of Eating Everything

After Wangechi Mutu

I toss my colossal head back and let it roll
open my wide mouth, it is glossed up and pussy
pink my face is a magazine in cuts like I said
I open my mouth after hunting and eat up
all the birds whole bird tribes, I enter
their murmuration and exit hemorrhage
it's whatever at first I look like a pretty girl
and then you see the giantess I've been I've eaten
everything I have kept no pet to love
my eyelids goldmelt I use my face to get
a little closer how the coyote changes its howl
at the canyon mouth and toward them come sweet
pups my belly lined with woolly afghans
from my grandmother's house and yours
even the front porch I've eaten I am nothing
but exhaust now I am puckered up and black
smoke rising I smile and anything surrenders
to this enormous don't they see me coming

Frasier Crane Toasts No One in Particular

To completing one rotation on the air

and falling into a bathtub of calendula

and orange peel

To unzipping my squash racquet

and hitting a volley beyond the oak tree

To shopping for a silk dressing gown, and then

giving it as a gift

To a dinner reservation my friends

could not have gotten

The opera, too

I've always loved a cortado

in the afternoon

an absolute, distilled with foamy

milk, but still, an absolute

I raise my tiny glass of sherry

were it fino or oloroso, I could tell you

without question

I've known just one irrepressible sound

and it's rainfall

My Beloved Finds Me Everywhere but Here

We are both poets

so I ask you

to write me into a poem

and you say: here, this one

is about shaping you

into a wave

or here

you are a horse

with lace reins

and I look

finding only music

or what could be

your mother so

I ask again *where am I*

and you say: who else

could I mean

when I write: sweet

witch, write: teeth you

say: can't you see it turn

like you do

Dishwashing the Mammy Salt & Pepper Shakers by Accident

two
    black faces
two
    housecoats
too-
    red mouths

two
    pairs of
too-
    white eyes
two
    porcelain sisters

into
    forgetting

On Injury

I break the window
         and climb into the passive

         night I'm a witch
         with two broken

feet but I'm a witch so
         what matters

even if all those bones
         break the little

ones I mean the fifth ones
         the ones that look

like they belong to field
         mice and lift water

toward my mouth even them
         are witch bones
so what

I guess I mean something
         about the body's irrelevance

or the fantasy of that

Bayuk

After Muddy Waters

As if I too were in the bayou   I kill a fly in my hands and stare
into the elm   blood from my cut
lip on a bottle   something moves and we call it Evenin'

rolling over in her slip of shade and nightsound   as if I too
were in the bayou   sweat lit under lantern   the body's tender
meridians   you close your teeth on   something bucks
in the switchgrass   who else but Evenin'

shaking loose   her blanket of prey   as if
I too were in the bayou how   first I rip tissue from the bone
then break its sweet horn

Bellum

If I take up the bow

What should we kill

How will we disappear

Behind the cypress

How will we

Convince them

We are gone

What will we call mercy

Is it the arrow

To the bloodline

Do we keep

Their names

Or call them

By our own

Pre-Earth and Post-Earth Life

Pre-earth was covered in snow. I told fibs.
I wanted my co-eternal God to love me more
than they loved everyone else. My ancestors
are imperfect. They don't always look upon
me in wonder. They were here too, engaging
in little vanities. Who then, do I turn to when
I want applause? When God knows the
truth already. What is it that they say God
is subject to? Continuous Revelation. It feels
like a loophole, but, it takes a lot to admit
when you're wrong.

Ars Poetica with Mother and Dogs

I turn and don't expect my mother's face
                    I ask *how did you enter this poem*
she says it wasn't easy

she is dressed in my favorite horse-print silk sheath
                    and dripping lake water
says she wore it to trick my lover

I want to ask *How could you* but instead
                    I reach behind her and break a vase
she used to love but we are surrounded

by dogs some of them used to sleep
                    at our bedsides but don't
anymore she grabs my hand and who am I anyway

to keep asking
                    her to leave why not take her face
and explain the damned line

Fear of Motherhood

Lucky, I've seen sea turtles slowly crawl out of a moonlit ocean
on their way to lay their eggs in the sand.
But I didn't feel a thing until, moved, I heard a stranger gasp.

Standing at the Sacré-Coeur—the one in Paris, and not in Idaho—
I've gazed upon La Ville Lumière under rain
and fretted about my long walk home.

I worry that when you're born I'll look at you like that.
Hoping you'll say OK, we can leave the concert before the last set,
just so that we don't get lost in the overwhelming crowd.

Visiting Whitney Plantation

Clouds hanging so low they almost touch
the wooden colonnettes of the big house
the brick, held together by animal
fur and mud, *bousillage*, the hands
that formed it. I raise my arm and rub
the belly of a cloud
our tour guide is Black and doesn't remark
on architectural flourishes. I am grateful
and still wiping sweat from my brow

We are in Wallace, Louisiana
looking for our people's names
now upon a marble wall of seventy thousand
first names in no particular order

I sidestep a white man with a camera
so that I can take my mother's
hand from her mouth and hold it

On the way to New Orleans we stop
to gather Spanish moss
A groundsman opens the gate after hours
he looks softly after my mother and me
could it be that he is one of us
I fill my purse with moss and unlock
the rental car

How cruel the sun must've been
to the slave, I think, when I get back
to our French Quarter hotel and lie
poolside in a two-piece
desperate, almost

Family Tree at Earth's Surface

After looking, and not looking without
using all the tools on the table:
expert, archive, attic, passed word, hunch, self
I come to Nameless mother and her son.
in one matter of seeing, they lived not
long ago, but for me, Unnamed
mother is just as well the moon, tidemaker.
Blackness does not begin there but first breaks
into a boy they call Jackson, leaver
of his last name, farmer, coffin builder.
Of course, we know there is another tool,
another knowing that we arc forever
an arc in which the moon herself
is affectionately mothered, and so
comforted, I lose the impulse to keep
counting, recording their names at all

Eden

I'm home, you could see me through
the kitchen window washing my daughter's dishes
my hands are busy but I'm looking at the elk
on the face of the mountain

I know nothing about elk, but here
we are, at any given moment
there must be countless allegories
but I'm only interested in one

am I home or am I only visiting? I am through
with asking, I'm at the center of a cul-de-sac
wind sweeps through the aspen like a hiss
we are in our own snow cup

melted to the summer people we really are
I am answering for myself
Hissssssssssss of the aspen, at the beginning
of which could, I suppose, be anything

cul-de-sac, just as well, a saucer, rising up,
up to the summit, it's possible I've never been
higher, I feel it, I'm really leaving now
moving through the told story

Acknowledgments

The Atlantic: "I Learn to Shoot a Bow"

BuzzFeed: "Visiting Whitney Plantation"

The Cortland Review: "North Node"

Huizache: "I'm Forced to Imagine There Are Two of Me Here"

Jai-Alai Magazine: "I Have Learned to Define a Field as a Space between Mountains," "Like a Suggestion," and "Writing Lately," an earlier version of "Ars Poetica with Mother and Dogs"

The Miami Rail: "Black Annie Hall" (annotated version)

The Offing: "Bellum" and "To Salt Lake, Letter Regarding Genealogy"

Poem-a-Day, Academy of American Poets: "Driving at Night"

Poetry Society of America: "UFO, for Instance"

Prairie Schooner: "Black Annie Hall"

Sugar House Review: "It's Like That Scene in *Annie Hall* Where Annie Leaves Her Body" and "Salt"

"Bayuk" appeared in *Chorus: A Literary Mixtape*, edited by Saul Williams, Gallery Books/MTV Books (2012)

"The End of Eating Everything," "Self-Portrait in a Tanning Bed," and "What Begets What Begets" appeared in *The BreakBeat Poets: Black Girl Magic*, edited by Mahogany L. Browne, Idrissa Simmonds, and Jamila Woods, Haymarket Books (2018)

"North Node" also appeared in *Bettering American Poetry 2015*, edited by Kenzie Allen, Eunsong Kim, Amy King, Jason Koo, Héctor Ramírez, Metta Sáma, Vanessa Angelica Villarreal, and Nikki Wallschlaeger, Bettering Books (2017)

*

To my family, small, and unlikely, and relentlessly supportive.

To my parents, for the bright light of their love, and for their example.

To Brian and Santi, who fill me with impossible joy and belonging.

To my many sisters: Katie Goldstein, Melissa Valentine, Rachelle Cruz, Arielle Lathan, Kelly Simpson, Jade Flower Foster, Andrea Marpillero-Colomina, and Daphne Amalia Rubin-Vega, for the gift of growing alongside you.

To the sweetest, and most unexpected, ecstatic sustained bonding with Ebony LaDelle, Nicole Counts, and Carla Bruce-Eddings.

To poets who've inspired me, mentored me, made me laugh, opened doors, poured cups, babysat, and lifted me up when, especially when, poetry has felt lost to me: Robin Coste Lewis, Zakia Henderson-Brown, Kyla Marshell, Keith Wilson, Kenyatta Rogers, Nicole Sealey, Mahogany L. Browne, Aldrin Valdez, Paul Tran, Ricardo Hernandez, Jayson Smith, Alison Roh Park, Morgan Parker, Tracie Morris, Suzanne Gardinier, Matthea Harvey, Tina Chang, Brenda Shaughnessy, Rachel Eliza Griffiths, Ross Gay, Sharon Olds, Terrance Hayes, Yusef Komunyakaa, Kevin Young, and Claudia Rankine.

To Cave Canem.

The poems in this collection were written with fellowship, vision, sacred space, and support from: the Good Times Collective; BLKGRP; the NYU Creative Writing Program; Sarah Lawrence College; Poets House; CantoMundo; O, Miami; the Schomburg Center for Research in Black Culture; the Jerome Foundation; the Highlights Foundation; the Family History Library; the Utah State Historical Society; Marya Spence; Patrick Nolan; Allie Merola; and Annika Karody.

And to the cinematic work of John Singleton, where I first heard the words of a poet, and after which I was forever changed.

Notes

"Far Enough": These words used by Bethel AME pastor Jerry Ford to honor Byrdie Lee Howell Langon are likely a rough quotation of a poem often attributed to Roy Croft, "Love," published in 1936. Byrdie Lee Howell Langon was the great-aunt of the author.

"North Node": "North node" is an astrological term, a lunar node, that represents the path one grows toward through life; it has also been referred to as a "north star."

"Like a Suggestion": Antelope Island is the largest of ten islands located within the Great Salt Lake in the state of Utah. It is well-known for its significant population of American bison, which were introduced to the island in 1893.

"Driving at Night": This poem is dedicated to Laquan McDonald. On October 20, 2014, Laquan McDonald, a seventeen-year-old Black teenager, was shot sixteen times within fourteen seconds by Jason Van Dyke, a thirty-six-year-old white officer with the Chicago Police Department.

"Salt": Brigham Young was a religious leader in the Mormon Church and the first governor of Utah. Latter-day Saints consider him to have been a prophet of God. In 1847 he conducted a pioneer company to the Rocky Mountains; when they arrived at the vista above Emigration Canyon, he is said to have proclaimed, "It is enough. This is the right place; drive on." Today, this location is memorialized as This Is the Place Heritage Park.

Sun Ra was an Afrofuturist jazz musician and poet who cowrote an eighty-five-minute science fiction film titled *Space Is the Place*, based, in part, on Sun Ra's lectures at UC Berkeley.

"Black Annie Hall": *Annie Hall* is a 1977 romantic comedy directed by disgraced predatory filmmaker Woody Allen and cowritten by Woody Allen and Marshall Brickman. Annie Hall was the name of the lead character in the film, played by actor Diane Keaton.

This poem subverts a scene from *Annie Hall* where the character Annie sees a theatrical showing of the film *The Sorrow and the Pity*, a two-part documentary about the collaboration of the Vichy government and Nazi Germany during World War II, by referencing a film called *Within Our Gates*, a 1920 silent film directed by Oscar Micheaux that portrays racial violence under white supremacy in the United

States during the early twentieth century. *Within Our Gates* is the oldest known surviving film made by a Black director.

"Black Mary Wilkie": Mary Wilkie is the lead character in the 1979 romantic comedy film *Manhattan*, directed by Woody Allen and cowritten by Woody Allen and Marshall Brickman.

This poem references the "watchtower," which refers to the large fluorescent sign at the former Brooklyn Heights headquarters of the Jehovah's Witnesses, visible across Manhattan's East River. The "watchtower" sign was visible from 1970 to 2017.

"Black Lead in a Nancy Meyers Film": Nancy Meyers is an American writer, director, and producer who is best known for her romantic comedies.

"Questions of the Last Relative Slave": This poem is dedicated to Paul Cephas Howell, born in 1855 and enslaved in DeSoto Parish, Louisiana. Paul later became the first Black police officer in the state of Utah and one of the first Black detectives in the United States. He is the second great-grandfather of the author.

"Écriture Féminine": "Écriture féminine," or "women's writing," is a term coined by French feminist and literary theorist Hélène Cixous in her 1975 essay "The Laugh of the Medusa."

"Black Frasier Crane": Frasier Crane was the lead character in an American sitcom called *Frasier*, set in Seattle, Washington, and centering the life of a radio psychiatrist. The show was broadcast for eleven seasons between 1993 and 2004.

"The End of Eating Everything": *The End of Eating Everything* is an animated video by Afrofuturist visual artist Wangechi Mutu.

Born and raised in Salt Lake City, Utah, Rio Cortez is the *New York Times* bestselling author of *The ABCs of Black History* (2020) and *I Have Learned to Define a Field As a Space Between Mountains,* winner of the 2015 Toi Derricotte and Cornelius Eady Chapbook Prize. Her honors include a *Poets & Writers* Amy Award as well as fellowships from Cave Canem, CantoMundo, the Jerome Foundation, and Poets House. Rio holds an MFA in creative writing from New York University.

PENGUIN POETS

GAROUS ABDOLMALEKIAN
Lean Against This Late Hour

PAIGE ACKERSON-KIELY
Dolefully, A Rampart Stands

JOHN ASHBERY
Selected Poems
Self-Portrait in a Convex Mirror

PAUL BEATTY
Joker, Joker, Deuce

JOSHUA BENNETT
Owed
The Sobbing School

TED BERRIGAN
The Sonnets

LAUREN BERRY
The Lifting Dress

JOE BONOMO
Installations

PHILIP BOOTH
Lifelines: Selected Poems 1950–1999
Selves

JIM CARROLL
Fear of Dreaming: The Selected Poems
Living at the Movies
Void of Course

RIO CORTEZ
Golden Ax

ALISON HAWTHORNE DEMING
Genius Loci
Rope
Stairway to Heaven

CARL DENNIS
Another Reason
Callings
Earthborn
New and Selected Poems 1974–2004
Night School
Practical Gods
Ranking the Wishes
Unknown Friends

DIANE DI PRIMA
Loba

STUART DISCHELL
Backwards Days
Dig Safe

STEPHEN DOBYNS
Velocities: New and Selected Poems 1966–1992

EDWARD DORN
Way More West

HEID E. ERDRICH
Little Big Bully

ROGER FANNING
The Middle Ages

ADAM FOULDS
The Broken Word: An Epic Poem of the British Empire in Kenya, and the Mau Mau Uprising Against It

CARRIE FOUNTAIN
Burn Lake
Instant Winner
The Life

AMY GERSTLER
Dearest Creature
Ghost Girl
Index of Women
Medicine
Nerve Storm
Scattered at Sea

EUGENE GLORIA
Drivers at the Short-Time Motel
Hoodlum Birds
My Favorite Warlord
Sightseer in This Killing City

DEBORA GREGER
In Darwin's Room

ZEINA HASHEM BECK
O

TERRANCE HAYES
American Sonnets for My Past and Future Assassin
Hip Logic
How to Be Drawn
Lighthead
Wind in a Box

NATHAN HOKS
The Narrow Circle

ROBERT HUNTER
Sentinel and Other Poems

MARY KARR
Viper Rum

WILLIAM KECKLER
Sanskrit of the Body

JACK KEROUAC
Book of Blues
Book of Haikus
Book of Sketches

JOANNA KLINK
Circadian
Excerpts from a Secret Prophecy
The Nightfields
Raptus

JOANNE KYGER
As Ever: Selected Poems

ANN LAUTERBACH
Hum
If in Time:
  Selected Poems
  1975–2000
On a Stair
Or to Begin Again
Spell
Under the Sign

CORINNE LEE
Plenty
Pyx

PHILLIS LEVIN
May Day
Mercury
Mr. Memory
  & Other Poems

PATRICIA LOCKWOOD
Motherland Fatherland
  Homelandsexuals

WILLIAM LOGAN
Rift of Light

J. MICHAEL MARTINEZ
Museum of the Americas

ADRIAN MATEJKA
The Big Smoke
Map to the Stars
Mixology
Somebody Else Sold
  the World

MICHAEL MCCLURE
Huge Dreams: San Francisco
  and Beat Poems

ROSE MCLARNEY
Forage
Its Day Being Gone

DAVID MELTZER
David's Copy:
  The Selected Poems
  of David Meltzer

TERESA K. MILLER
Borderline Fortune

ROBERT MORGAN
Dark Energy
Terroir

CAROL MUSKE-DUKES
An Octave Above Thunder:
  New and Selected Poems
Red Trousseau
Blue Rose
Twin Cities

ALICE NOTLEY
Certain Magical Acts
Culture of One
The Descent of Alette
Disobedience
For the Ride
In the Pines
Mysteries of Small Houses

WILLIE PERDOMO
The Crazy Bunch
The Essential Hits
  of Shorty Bon Bon

DANIEL POPPICK
Fear of Description

LIA PURPURA
It Shouldn't Have Been
  Beautiful

LAWRENCE RAAB
The History of Forgetting

BARBARA RAS
The Last Skin
One Hidden Stuff

MICHAEL ROBBINS
Alien vs. Predator
The Second Sex
Walkman

PATTIANN ROGERS
Generations
Holy Heathen Rhapsody
Quickening Fields
Wayfare

SAM SAX
Madness

ROBYN SCHIFF
A Woman of Property

WILLIAM STOBB
Absentia
Nervous Systems

TRYFON TOLIDES
An Almost Pure Empty
  Walking

VINCENT TORO
Tertulia

PAUL TRAN
All the Flowers Kneeling

SARAH VAP
Viability

ANNE WALDMAN
Gossamurmur
Kill or Cure
Manatee/Humanity
Trickster Feminism

JAMES WELCH
Riding the Earthboy 40

PHILIP WHALEN
Overtime: Selected Poems

PHILLIP B. WILLIAMS
Mutiny

ROBERT WRIGLEY
Anatomy of Melancholy
  and Other Poems
Beautiful Country
Box
Earthly Meditations:
  New and Selected Poems
Lives of the Animals
Reign of Snakes
The True Account of Myself
  as a Bird

MARK YAKICH
The Importance of Peeling
  Potatoes in Ukraine
Spiritual Exercises
Unrelated Individuals
  Forming a Group Waiting
  to Cross